CW00434150

G. K. Chesterton

by
Karl Schmude

*All booklets are published thanks to the
generous support of the members of the
Catholic Truth Society*

CATHOLIC TRUTH SOCIETY
PUBLISHERS TO THE HOLY SEE

Contents

Presented by the
Catholic Truth Society
to delegates of the
Chesterton Institute Conference 2012

Introduction

The reputation of G. K. Chesterton has not escaped the fate of most famous authors after their death – that of dwindling from a mass readership to the level of more spasmodic attention.

At the same time it is difficult to call a writer neglected who attracts notice as often as Chesterton, particularly in the form of quotations from his works, and whose books are regularly reprinted. The scintillation and depth of his thought, the freshness of his expression, the liveliness of his humour - all converge to explain the survival and permanent relevance of a man who, as Anthony Burgess has written, "knew what it was like to live on the level of eternity".[1]

It was the opinion of the English literary critic, Frank Swinnerton, that Chesterton's gifts would not be fully realised and acknowledged until at least a century had passed.[2] So immersed was he in the controversies of his day that, in so far as they have abated and passed out of memory, he has become inaccessible - and, in some respects, perhaps dated. Yet there remains a vast proportion of his work which is uneroded by time, and in which his thought is as vibrant and timely as it was in his own day.

The Roots of Genius

Childhood and education

Gilbert Keith Chesterton was born in London on 29th May, 1874. His father was a prosperous London auctioneer, and the young Chesterton developed a love for the charm and glory of England's celebrated capital city, where he lived until the age of thirty-five.

From his earliest years he enjoyed fairy tales, and his childhood delight in these stories evolved into an intellectual appreciation of their value. In one of the many essays which he wrote on this subject, he contended that the idea which is the core of morality is also the core of the nursery tales - the idea that peace and happiness can only exist on some condition.

> "Cinderella may have a dress woven on supernatural looms and blazing with unearthly brilliance; but she must be back when the clock strikes twelve. . . A girl is given a box on condition she does not open it; she opens it, and all the evils of this world rush out at her. A man and woman are put in a garden on condition that they do not eat one fruit: they eat it, and lose their joy in all the fruits of the earth."[3]

In Chesterton's view, all ethics should be taught to this fairy tale tune: "that, if one does the thing forbidden, one imperils all the things provided."[4] A whole chapter of the great work of his maturity, **Orthodoxy** (1908), is devoted to "The Ethics of Elfland", and explains how the truth about goodness and happiness came to him from nursery tales and formed the first basis of his philosophy.

In his **Autobiography** - his last book published several months after his death in June 1936 - Chesterton depicts his childhood with a sensibility and insight perhaps unsurpassed in modern literature. He recalls not only the incidents of this period, but also the thoughts and feelings which a child experiences. He displays a deep intuitive understanding of the way a child forms his picture of the world, and, as John Gross commented in a review of the **Autobiography** when it was reprinted in 1969, "his opening chapters are littered with sound observations and shrewd distinctions which are still worth pondering, notably in connection with the nature of play and the difference between imagination and illusion".[5]

A continuity of theme is as discernible in Chesterton's life as it is in his thought; a development as well, no doubt, but one which built upon the spiritual and emotional foundations of his childhood, deepening and not denying this early experience.

In 1887 he was enrolled at St. Paul's School in London. His five years there did not reveal him as a distinguished pupil. He seemed, indeed, to be backward in some respects: he did not talk until the age of three nor read until he was eight. He was often vague and absent-minded, and his teachers commonly judged him dull. Only one of his masters discerned the intellectual power which was soon to ripen. "Six foot of genius," remarked the teacher to his mother. "Cherish him, Mrs. Chesterton, cherish him."[6]

In fact, his puzzlement and confusion at this time concealed a serious search for life's meaning. "We felt," said one of his friends, "that he was looking for God".[7]

In 1892 Chesterton went to study at the Slade School of Art. He had always displayed a facility for drawing, and his three years as an art student developed this talent as well as strengthening a power which manifested itself later in his writing - a depth of vision. His first published works comprised poetry and art criticism, two literary forms which especially require a gift of imaginative vision.

Early writings

In 1900 he produced **Greybeards at Play** and **The Wild Knight and other Poems**, two volumes of verse which established his reputation as an author of unmistakable promise. His literary gifts had led him in 1895 to leave the art school and join a publisher's office, from where he soon ventured into freelance journalism. Throughout his life Chesterton regarded himself, first and foremost, as a journalist. He was, indeed, more a man of letters than a journalist in the currently received sense of the word. He lived to see journalism reduced from a profession to a trade, and a journalist become, as Chesterton himself put it, "a man who writes things on the back of advertisements".[8]

Chesterton, on the other hand, wrote what he liked on an endless array of topics, professing no expertise beyond that of the ordinary educated man. His first major prose work, **The Defendant** (1901), was a series of casual essays on certain ideas or attitudes commonly regarded as indefensible. "I have conceived," he wrote, "that a defendant is chiefly required when worldlings despise the world - that a counsel for the defence would not have been out of place in that terrible day when the sun was darkened over Calvary and Man was rejected of men".[9] Thus, Chesterton produced a plea for "patriotism", "humility", "baby-worship", and "detective stories". It was the beginning of a long and noble struggle for ideas and values which are now often derided; and it was the first of numerous books of essays which, under the guise of flippancy, explored profound truths about life. **Tremendous Trifles** (1909), **A Shilling for My Thoughts** (1916), **The Uses of Diversity** (1920), **Generally Speaking** (1928), **Come to Think of It** (1930) - these are some of the works which reveal Chesterton's great gifts as an essayist - a fertile imagination, a vivid style, an unquenchable interest in the world - as well as his vast capacity for perceiving the meaning of objects and attitudes now veiled by familiarity.

Had Chesterton lived to witness man's exploration of outer space, I fancy he might have observed that the chief reason for travelling to the moon should be to discover the earth. The remark would have been typically Chestertonian, for it was one of the cardinal principles of his thought that the best way to appreciate anything familiar in life is to discover it again; that one can grow so inured to something that its essential worth is lost to view, and that only by an immense jolt of the imagination can one again see it as it really is.

Chesterton had, as Ronald Knox noted in the panegyric at his Requiem Mass, "the artist's eye which could suddenly see in some quite familiar object a new value; he had the poet's intuition which could suddenly detect, in the tritest of phrases, a wealth of new meanings and of possibilities".[10] The wonders of the world had unaccountably been numbered at seven: Chesterton reckoned them unlimited.

> "Nearly all the best and most precious things in the universe you can get for a halfpenny. I make an exception, of course, of the sun, the moon, the earth, people, stars, thunderstorms, and such trifles. You can get them for nothing."[11]

When Samuel Johnson remarked that men more frequently require to be reminded than informed, he enunciated a truth which, over two centuries later, Chesterton was to demonstrate constantly. The most salient quality of his writing is this gift for renewing our vision of the realities and values which familiarity has betrayed us into neglecting.

In **The Napoleon of Notting Hill** (1904), the first of eleven novels and books of short stories - such as **The Man Who Was Thursday** (1908), **The Flying Inn** (1914), and **The Return of Don Quixote** (1927) - Chesterton describes how, in a burst of imaginative vision, one of his characters saw two friends, whom he found habitually dull, in a new and exciting light. There is a law, comments Chesterton, in the darkest of the books of life, and it is this: If you look at a thing nine hundred and ninety-nine times, you are perfectly safe; if you look at it the thousandth time, you are in frightful danger of seeing it for the first time.

Chesterton's Worldview

The Nature of wonder

In Chesterton's experience, the world abounded in surprises. "A man," he averred, "may very well be exasperated with London, as he may be with the universe; but in both cases he has no business to be bored with it."[12] Miracles surround us - the miracle of sequence, as the novelist Bruce Marshall once observed, being even more marvellous than the miracle of the interruption of the same sequence.[13] "From the beginning," Chesterton once told a reporter, "I think I was staggered by the stupendous marvel of existence - by the miracle of sunlight coming through a window, by the miracle of people walking on legs through the streets, by the miracle of people talking to each other."[14] The impression of monotony in life is a false impression - as destructive of the natural as of the supernatural order.

"Of one thing I am certain," Chesterton wrote early in his journalistic career, "that the age needs, first and foremost, to be startled; to be taught the nature of wonder."[15] It is almost a statement of his life's work. When he went to America in 1919 on the first of his two visits, he looked upon the lights of Broadway flashing out their message that man does indeed live by bread alone. "What a glorious garden of wonders this would be," he mused, "to any one who was lucky enough to be unable to read."[16]

This capacity to see what is too plain to be seen, to grasp the wonder of life despite the numbing influence of everyday experience, characterized Chesterton's whole mental outlook and inspired much of his writing.

Love of ordinary people

In the first place, it gave him an affinity with everyday life and the world of ordinary people. He did not see the common man as leading a life of irredeemable boredom and futility. On the contrary, he thought he had an indispensable part to play and a huge responsibility to bear, both in the family and in the society at large, and that the extravagant recognition accorded the expert in our time - in particular in fields beyond the expert's competence - threatened the stability and happiness of human society.

In "The Twelve Men", a famous essay on his experience as a juryman, Chesterton applauded the wisdom of asking ordinary people to pass judgment on their fellow human beings.

"Our civilization has decided, and very justly decided, that determining the guilt or innocence of men is a thing too important to be trusted to trained men. It wishes for light upon that awful matter, it asks men who know no more law than I know, but who can feel the things that I felt in the jury box. When it wants a library catalogued, or the solar system discovered, or any trifle of that kind, it uses up its specialists. But when it wishes anything done which is really serious, it collects twelve of the ordinary men standing round. The same thing was done, if I remember right, by the Founder of Christianity."[17]

No one understood the common man better than Chesterton; no one had a deeper appreciation of his loves and hungers. All his life he fought, through his writings, for the freedom and dignity, the normal loyalties and elementary rights of the ordinary person. Unlike many revolutionaries and reformers, Chesterton understood the people about whom he talked and for whom he professed to speak; his popular sympathies, as he wrote of his brother, Cecil, could really survive any intimacy with the populace.[18]

When Maisie Ward, founder with her Australian husband, Frank Sheed, of the publishing house of Sheed and Ward, produced a sequel to her biography of Chesterton,[19] it was filled with memories of the man, cherished not only by the great but also by the ordinary people who had been his friends - the secretaries who had worked for him, the barbers who had shaved him, the taximen who had transported him. In one essay he defined poets as "those who rise above the people by understanding them".[20] Only in this way could true leadership develop; only on this basis could genuine hope flourish.

Cherishing man, not superman

Many prophets in Chesterton's day based their social solutions upon despair of man - a tendency which has persisted to our own time, when proposals for population control and environmental conservation tend to betray an anti-human mentality, reflecting a loss of hope in man and in man's capacity to cooperate with God in handling life's problems.[21]

Chesterton, however, did not despair of man, and this was the fundamental ground of his disagreement with his lifelong friend and antagonist, George Bernard Shaw. Shaw's philosophy, in Chesterton's view, was that of a man utterly detached from human proceedings, unable to enter into the feelings and motives of ordinary people in spite of a genuine concern and zeal for their welfare. Shaw seemed to criticize human nature as if he himself did not possess it. His hope for an exceptional being who would never be cruel or nasty or narrow-minded, who would not give rise to disillusionment, was itself based on despair. "Hope for the superman," Chesterton declared, "is another name for despair of man".[22]

In contrast, Chesterton was impelled by a buoyant sense of hope. At first, this was a natural rather than a supernatural hope; a feeling of cosmic optimism, not an outlook rooted in divine faith and expressed in charity. At this stage Chesterton harboured a profound love of creation, a fundamental loyalty to life. Love and loyalty in turn excited gratitude, and to Chesterton the test of all happiness was gratitude.

> "Children are grateful when Santa Claus puts in their stockings gifts of toys or sweets. Could I not be grateful to Santa Claus when he put in my stockings the gift of two miraculous legs? We thank people for birthday presents of cigars and slippers. Can I thank no one for the birthday present of birth?"[23]

Only a man of deeply religious instincts could conceivably profess such an attitude. Chesterton was unquestionably such a man, but the faith which develops and fulfils those instincts had almost deserted him in adolescence. "I was a pagan," he confessed, "at the age of twelve, and a complete agnostic by the age of sixteen."[24] Even during this period, however, it was his sense of wonder, and his consequent sense of loyalty and gratitude, which sustained him. "I hung on to religion," he recalled, "by one thin thread of thanks."[25]

At the same time, Chesterton was conscious that this outlook could easily produce a false optimism. The optimism of the world, he came to realise, is false, because it is always trying to prove that we fit into the world. Christian optimism, on the other hand, is based on the fact that we do *not* fit into the world; that our ultimate destiny lies elsewhere; and that we can feel homesick - even when we are at home. As C. S. Lewis, who was vitally influenced by Chesterton, once observed: "If I find in myself a desire which no experience in this world can satisfy, the most probable explanation is that I was made for another world."[26]

Orthodoxy and the excitement of truth

Thus for Chesterton, the central challenge was to evolve a view of life which combined this sense of strangeness in the world with a sense of loyalty to it. The trap of judging and valuing the world in its own terms and by its own standards had to be avoided, for Chesterton knew that such a course would imprison him in a self-contained universe amid a self-centred humanity, and this - the essential character of a secularized culture closed to spiritual influence - could never satisfy the yearnings of the human spirit. One must, he realised, somehow find a way of loving the world without trusting it; loving the world without becoming worldly. It was in Christianity that he found the solution, and in 1908 he outlined his intellectual and spiritual odyssey in what is indisputably one of his greatest books, **Orthodoxy**.

It is remarkable that even Chesterton should have been able to produce such a work at the age of thirty-five; but it is supremely characteristic of his other-worldliness that he sold the rights of the book for £100 - an action so recklessly unbusinesslike that it shocked, not for the last time, the astute commercial instincts of Bernard Shaw.

A century has now passed since **Orthodoxy** first appeared, yet it remains an extraordinarily striking work. For several decades after its publication, it registered a profound impact, and it is astonishing how many Catholics have acknowledged its influence on their conversion. In the 1960s, the distinguished British diplomat, Sir Alec Randall, recalled that the book proved with him, "as I know it did with many others," an important stage in his progress to the Catholic Church.[27] More recently, the young American writer Dawn Eden attributes her conversion to reading **The Man Who Was Thursday** and **Orthodoxy**, and finding in Chesterton a way out of the crevasse of sexual permissiveness into which the culture of the 1960s had plunged her.[28]

Orthodoxy presented a new and excitingly adventurous outline of Christian truth. No longer was it credible for the sceptic to presume, as he had done for so long, that the historic Faith was humdrum and debilitating. Chesterton had shown it to be a "thrilling romance", and in one chapter, "The Paradoxes of

Christianity", he provided a rousing depiction of its progress through history.

> "The orthodox Church never took the tame course or accepted the conventions; the orthodox Church was never respectable. It would have been easier to have accepted the earthly power of the Arians. It would have been easy, in the Calvinistic seventeenth century, to fall into the bottomless pit of predestination. It is easy to be a madman: it is easy to be a heretic. It is always easy to let the age have its head; the difficult thing is to keep one's own. It is always easy to be a modernist; as it is easy to be a snob. To have fallen into any of those open traps of error and exaggeration which fashion after fashion and sect after sect set along the historic path of Christendom – that would indeed have been simple. It is always simple to fall; there are an infinity of angles at which one falls, only one at which one stands. ·To have fallen into any one of the fads from Gnosticism to Christian Science would indeed have been obvious and tame. But to have avoided them all has been one whirling adventure; and in my vision the heavenly chariot flies thundering through the ages, the dull heresies sprawling and prostrate, the wild truth reeling but erect."[29]

The man who at one time trained to be an artist had manifestly found his forte: he was an artist in words.

Heresy and the distortion of truth

Orthodoxy appeared three years after a book to which it was a counterpart - **Heretics** (1905). In that work Chesterton examined, and found wanting, the philosophies of certain notable contemporaries, such as Rudyard Kipling, H. G. Wells and Bernard Shaw. He regarded them all as aspiring prophets who had lapsed into heresy - by emphasizing one aspect of truth and ignoring others. Indeed, this is how, in Chesterton's judgment, such men came to be regarded as prophets. It was thought that each had discovered a new and breathtaking idea: whereas, in fact, what was new was not the idea, but only the *isolation* of the idea. It had been dragged from its context and magnified, made to appear the whole truth, but with the catastrophic result that the balance and unity of truth were disturbed, and the elements of truth were steadily and successively denied, leading to a distortion of truth itself. Thus, an exclusive concentration on the mercy of God can lead to a neglect of His justice; or the denial of man as an image of God, of a human nature which is fixed and inherited from God, leads inexorably to the denial of human life itself - in the forms of abortion, sterilization, euthanasia, and other evils.

Chesterton admitted that he, on his part, had been tempted to be a popular kind of prophet. "I did try," he declared, "to found a heresy of my own; and when I had put the last touches to it, I discovered that it was orthodoxy."[30] The same unnerving discovery was made by Chesterton's contemporary and friend, the artist, Eric Gill (1882-1940), who devised his own religion and then found that the Catholic Church was the exact embodiment of it. In later life, Chesterton realised that, "in becoming more and more solidly certain of such a thing as a truth, one loses the temptation to exaggerate it as a challenge".[31] He realised, further, that the heretic is not, as is commonly thought, a man who loves truth too much; no man can love truth too much. The heretic is a man who loves his truth more than truth itself. He prefers the half-truth that he has found to the whole truth which humanity has found.[32] In consequence, a heresy always impressed Chesterton as a restriction, not a liberation; a lopping off of a part of the truth - and therefore, ultimately, a loss of liberty. For it is only the truth which can make us free.

Christian Hope

The fall of man and Christian hope

Among the truths which Christianity taught and had transmitted, the doctrine of the Fall of Man was strongly appealing to Chesterton's mind. Although unfashionable in contemporary culture, the notion that the human race is, in Newman's words, "implicated in some terrible aboriginal calamity," which renders it "out of joint with the purposes of its Creator,"[33] is, as Chesterton saw it, the only encouraging view of life. "It holds," as he maintained in perhaps his greatest book of apologetic essays, **The Thing** (1929), ". . . that we have misused a good world, and not merely been entrapped into a bad one. It refers evil back to the wrong use of the will, and thus declares that it can eventually be righted by the right use of the will. Every other creed except that one is some form of surrender to fate."[34]

Chesterton dwelt frequently upon the Fall of Man, for he saw the doctrine as being indispensable to a true grasp of human experience, and central to an understanding of Christian hope. Nowhere was his brilliance as a Christian apologist more singularly evident than in his unfolding of the concept of original sin. We speak, he once noted, of a manly man, but not of a whaley whale.

"If you wanted to dissuade a man from drinking his tenth whisky, you would slap him on the back and say, 'Be a man.' No one who wished to dissuade a crocodile from eating his tenth explorer would slap it on the back and say, 'Be a crocodile.' For we have no notion of a perfect crocodile; no allegory of a whale expelled from his whaley Eden."[35]

Thus, Chesterton perceived that God's gift of life was good, but that man had violated the conditions of the gift. The salient lesson of the fairy tales, which Chesterton imbibed as a child, had become a central feature of his intellectual outlook as an adult.

"God had written, not so much a poem, but rather a play; a play he had planned as perfect, but which had necessarily been left to human actors and stage-managers, who had since made a great mess of it."[36]

Many years later, Chesterton was to write a play on this very theme. **The Surprise**, written around 1930 but not published until 1952, presented a dramatic action in which, at the outset, the author's plot was exactly followed by the characters, who were played first by puppets, so that his intention was perfectly fulfilled. In the Second Act, however, the characters are played by living men and women who, tempted to depart from the plot, consequently make havoc of the play.

The author is goaded beyond endurance. "What do you think you are doing with my play?" he cries out from the wings. "Drop it! Stop! I am coming down."[37] Here was Chesterton's depiction of the central Christian paradox - the author invading the stage, the creator visiting his people to reveal his purposes. Here was an imaginative unfolding of the central message of **Orthodoxy**.

Orthodoxy had been written to show what the modern prophets were heretics from. In an essay published only a year before he died, Chesterton explained his use of the word. He defined orthodoxy as "that primary principle, or right reason in things, by which they can be judged independently of new fads or of old prejudices".[38] The orthodox truth may be new or it may be old, but it is not true for either of these reasons. The Christian, continued Chesterton, "is not intrinsically intolerant of things that are new and revolutionary, being well aware that he was once new and revolutionary himself". Yet on the other hand, "even when there is a truth in tradition, we must still distinguish between the tradition and the truth".[39]

Objective truth

The philosophy which Chesterton embraced was the traditional Christian faith; but he did not embrace it because it was traditional, he embraced it because it was true.

For our time, perhaps the most pertinent quality of **Orthodoxy** is its unswervingly objective approach to truth. Though Chesterton undoubtedly responded to his own deeply felt need for an explanation of life, he did not conduct his search along those lines. He did not derive his philosophy from his own inner experience, as if this were an infallible response to objective reality; above all did he avoid being guided uncritically by what Sir Arnold Lunn called an "fif", a "funny internal feeling", which Lunn criticised as the most common basis for contemporary thought and behaviour.[40] Chesterton grounded his thought in experience outside himself, relating it to circumstances and standards that are universally recognizable. Hence, his philosophy was not a personal philosophy in the sense that it was unique to him and incommunicable. "God and humanity made it," he said, "and it made me".[41]

Few writers in the past century have argued more persuasively for an objective approach to philosophic truth. Pride he once defined as "the falsification of fact by the introduction of self." In order to learn, he claimed, a man must "subtract *himself* from the study of any solid and objective thing".[42] Chesterton remained perpetually alive to the dangers of subjectivism. "A cosmic philosophy." he pointed out, "is not constructed to fit a man; a cosmic philosophy is constructed to fit a cosmos. A man can no more possess a private religion than he can possess a private sun and moon."[43]

In answer to those who were prone to obscure the objective difference between right and wrong, Chesterton asked:

> "Supposing there is no difference between good and bad, or between false and true, what is the difference between up and down?"[44]

Conversion to Catholicism

It is a fact sufficiently remarkable that Chesterton did not enter the Catholic Church until 1922. The explanation for the delay, in so far as the mystery of faith is open to human understanding, seems to have been more personal than intellectual. Scarcely any mental obstacles remained in his path to Rome; even the matter of spiritual authority, and the Church as the earthly repository of that authority - an issue over which many potential converts have agonized - did not present difficulties. To Chesterton it was perfectly reasonable that the Church which Christ had founded should speak with the same authority as Christ Himself did when on earth.

Yet in the final analysis, conversion is a matter of grace rather than reason, a conclusion of the will and not merely a conclusion of the mind; and Chesterton, whose mind was so unimaginably swift, was fairly slow to act. Moreover, in this momentous decision, he was inhibited further by the fact that his beloved wife, Frances, could not accompany him. Married in 1901, the Chestertons were intensely devoted to each other, and it was Frances, a dedicated Anglican, who helped to revive Chesterton's interest in religion; just as it was Our Lady who helped him in his subsequent conversion to Catholicism. Frances herself was received into the Catholic Church in 1926, four years after her husband.

To Chesterton, conversion was truly a rebirth, and the beautiful sonnet which he wrote on the occasion expressed this reality:

> The sages have a hundred maps to give
> That trace their crawling cosmos like a tree,
> They rattle reason out through many a sieve
> That stores the sand and lets the gold go free:
> And all these things are less than dust to me
> Because my name is Lazarus and I live.[45]

Four years were to elapse before Chesterton published an account of his conversion. **The Catholic Church and Conversion** is a persuasive piece of apologetics, in which the author insists that he could justify the whole of Catholic theology, provided that he is allowed to use the two ideas which the Church is popularly presumed to forbid: reason and liberty. In the face of the fundamental doubts of our time, Chesterton affirmed that the Catholic "alone will have freedom, that he alone will have will, because he alone will believe in free will; that he alone will have reason, since ultimate doubt denies reason as well as authority; that he alone will truly act, because action is performed to an end".[46] Increasingly did Chesterton recognize that "there is one Church exactly as there is one universe; and no wise man will wander about looking for another."[47]

A Prolific Career

Chesterton the aphorist and journalist

Chesterton's gift for framing the unforgettable phrase, the quotable quote, is a celebrated one. Like Shakespeare, his work seems to be full of quotations! In the **Viking Book of Aphorisms** which W. H. Auden and Louis Kronenberger compiled in 1962, Chesterton was impressively represented - ranking with such authors as Goethe and Samuel Johnson. Auden has elsewhere pronounced him "without any doubt one of the finest aphorists in English literature".[48] A sharpness of mind, an intuitive sense of reality, a rare capacity for focusing on two truths at the one time - a capacity which led to the paradoxes for which Chesterton was renowned, or, as some thought, notorious - all these qualities made him a born journalist, writing for his own time, as well as a great philosopher, writing for all time.

T. S. Eliot once stated that the commentator's task is "to find the topical excuse for writing about the permanent."[49] It was a vocation which Chesterton naturally pursued, though it was one that he found increasingly burdensome as he grew older.

Many of his greatest books were composed of articles which first appeared in periodical form. **Orthodoxy** was the crown and fulfilment of certain ideas which Chesterton rehearsed in 1903-4 during a lengthy debate on Christianity in the **Clarion**, a Socialist weekly of the period; some contributions to **Blackfriars** in 1922-3 formed the basis of a number of important chapters in **The Everlasting Man** (1925); while his superb biography of **St Francis of Assisi** (1923) arose from a whole series of disparate writings - schoolboy verses, an essay on the saint in **Twelve Types** (1902), and several articles in the **Daily News** - produced over a period of years.

The complaint has often been made that Chesterton wrote too much and too variously, and in particular that he devoted too much time to journalism. Assuredly his output was prodigious. He wrote some one hundred books and contributed introductions to another hundred - or, as he put it when these introductions were later collected into one volume, they were "prefaces to which other people have fervently contributed excellent books."[50] He wrote regularly for a host of periodicals, notably the **Daily News**, the **Eye Witness** (a weekly journal launched in 1911 by Chesterton's brother, Cecil, and Hilaire Belloc), and the **Illustrated London News**. For the latter alone he produced more than sixteen hundred essays, for he contributed a weekly article from 1905 to 1936, and these are being progressively consolidated as part of the Ignatius Press edition of his *Collected Works*.

So fertile was his genius that, in one decade at the summit of his creative powers (1904-1914), he wrote twenty-six books. They embrace every form of literature - novels, poetry, essays, literary criticism, plays, philosophical tracts and detective stories. Only a severe illness which struck him in 1914, and nearly ended his life, curbed this stupendous flow of writing.

The Father Brown stories

It was during this period that the Father Brown stories began to appear. Of all of Chesterton's works, these stories have proved to be the most popular. From 1911, when **The Innocence of Father Brown** appeared, until 1935, when a final collection of the stories, entitled **The Scandal of Father Brown**, was published, these detective tales continued to pour out from Chesterton's pen. In the opinion of the English novelist, Kingsley Amis, they are in the finest detective-story tradition. "They are more than that," he states. "They are models, helping to shape that tradition as well as adding lustre to it."[51]

The character of Father Brown was based upon a Yorkshire priest, Monsignor John O'Connor, who was a great friend of Chesterton and in 1922 received him into the Catholic Church.[52] Monsignor O'Connor revealed to Chesterton that unworldliness can be perfectly compatible with a knowledge of the world - above all, of the underworld of crime and wickedness. The insights into human nature, sharpened especially by the experience of the confessional, could be guaranteed to expose a priest to the full reality of human failings. Thus, Father Brown possessed a special insight into human minds and hearts. He could think like the criminal because he understood him at a deep level; and, therefore, he could anticipate what the criminal planned to do, or determine who among various individuals *was* the criminal.

At the same time, Chesterton was at pains to make clear that Father Brown was an ordinary man - an extraordinarily ordinary man, no doubt, like Chesterton himself - but nonetheless, a man with normal human tendencies and weaknesses. Indeed, this is Chesterton's outstanding achievement with the Father Brown stories. As one critic has argued, he turns what is an inherent limitation of the detective story - namely, that no character can have much depth, or receive much delineation, because all must be potential suspects - into a strength, for Chesterton created a setting which reveals the universal human potentiality of guilt and sin.[53] Father Brown was able to identify himself with the criminal because he, being a man, contained this potentiality within himself. "Are you a devil?" the exposed criminal asked. "I am a man," replied Father Brown, "and therefore have all devils in my heart".[54]

One of the most memorable features of the Father Brown stories is Chesterton's descriptions of landscapes. They show, firstly, that he was a consummate writer, and secondly, that his imagination was intensely visual, for the painter's eye can be found in all his descriptions.

"They pushed slowly up the brightening river; the glowing violet of the sky and the pale gold of the moon grew fainter and fainter, and faded into that vast colourless cosmos that precedes the colours of the dawn. When the first faint stripes of red and gold and grey split the horizon from end to end they were broken by the black bulk of a town or village which sat on the river just ahead of them. It was already an easy twilight, in which all things were visible, when they came under the hanging roofs and bridges of this riverside hamlet. The houses, with their long, low, stooping roofs, seemed to come down to drink at the river, like huge grey and red cattle. The broadening and whitening dawn had already turned to working daylight before they saw any living creature on the wharves and bridges of that silent town."[55]

Chesterton the critic

Such passages point to the literary critic in Chesterton, the power of acute observation combined with verbal sensitivity. Among his earliest books were literary studies

- of the artist, G. F. Watts (1902) and of Robert Browning (1903) - and it was clear from the popular reaction to these works that an unusually perceptive critic had arrived on the literary scene. The Browning volume in particular was acclaimed as one of the most illuminating interpretations of the poet that had yet been written.

Chesterton excelled at the first function of any critic - that of extending the grounds on which an author or work can be enjoyed. He argued that an inferior appreciation sends the reader to his hundredth reading of a work, whereas the higher appreciation sends him to his first reading of it.[56] As in so many other spheres, Chesterton enlarged our powers of vision in the realm of literature. He stimulated what he called "the most wild and soaring sort of imagination: the imagination that can see what is there".[57]

As well as the studies of Watts and Browning, Chesterton wrote literary biographies of Charles Dickens (1906), Bernard Shaw (1909), William Blake (1910), William Cobbett (1925), Robert Louis Stevenson (1927), and Chaucer (1932). In addition, he penned a volume on the **Victorian Age in Literature**, which, though unlike the usual histories of literature, roused widespread admiration for its insights into Victorian writing. In particular, he demonstrated the effect of the Victorian compromise between religion and rationalism on the literature of the period.

"The difference that the period had developed can best be seen if we consider this: that while neither was of a spiritual sort, Macaulay took it for granted that common sense required some kind of theology, while Huxley took it for granted that common sense meant having none. Macaulay, it is said, never talked about his religion: but Huxley was always talking about the religion he hadn't got."[58]

Chesterton the editor

Many of Chesterton's admirers have expressed regret, at different times, that he did not concentrate upon literature, but instead dissipated his vast talents in unending journalism. Christopher Hollis, for instance, has lamented his assuming the editorship of the **Eye Witness** from his brother, Cecil.

Born five years after Gilbert, Cecil very soon began to engage with his brother in interminable debate: "we perpetually argued," recalled Gilbert, but "never quarrelled".[59] Cecil possessed a fierceness of character and abrasiveness of style notably absent in his elder brother. Desmond MacCarthy called Cecil "the best pugnacious journalist since Cobbett".[60] There is no doubt that the two brothers were decidedly different. Yet the love between them was deep and indestructible: and when Cecil, who fought during the First World War, died tragically at the age of thirty-nine a few days after the

Armistice of 1918, Gilbert felt duty-bound to assume the journalistic struggle which Cecil, as a political journalist, had more naturally borne. In Gilbert's mind,

> "[Cecil] lived long enough to march to the victory which was for him a supreme vision of liberty and the light. The work which he put first he did before he died. The work which he put second, but very near to the other, he left for us to do. There are many of us who will abandon many other things, and recognize no greater duty than to do it."[61]

Gilbert recognized no greater duty than to take over the editorship of the paper which Cecil had begun in association with Hilaire Belloc. Renamed the **New Witness** by Cecil in 1912, the paper eventually became - much in defiance of Chesterton's essential modesty - **G. K.'s Weekly**. Its objects were, firstly, to expose political corruption and denounce the system by which contributions to party funds procured titles of honour - Chesterton once said that the rich man pays into party funds and becomes a knight, while the poor man is paid out of party funds and becomes a slave - and secondly, to disseminate the principles of Distributism, which was a social scheme for the widest possible distribution of property, formulated in the tradition of the papal encyclicals on social justice.

Chesterton's Social Thought

Distributism and social freedom

Distributism was conceived as a social remedy, both for the concentration of property in the hands of a rich minority (the capitalist solution) and for the control of property by the State (the socialist solution). Under capitalism and communism, the two seeming antinomies, declared Chesterton wittily, the normal man is not minding his own business, but somebody else's.

The normal man - this was the starting-point of Chesterton's sociology, just as God was the starting-point of his theology. He thought it futile to judge what social institutions would work for man until it had first been decided what is the nature of man; futile to discuss such questions as the object of education until it had been determined what is the object of man.

Chesterton's conception of human society began, continued and ended with his sympathy and respect for man - "the old, unaltered, fighting, beer-drinking, creed-making, child-loving, affectionate, selfish, unreasonable, respectable man".[62] The things that have been founded on this creature, thought Chesterton, immortally remain; the things that have been founded on the image of the perfect man, the 'Superman', have died with the dying civilisations which alone have given them birth.

> "When Christ at a symbolic moment was establishing His great society, He chose for its corner-stone neither the brilliant Paul nor the mystic John, but a shuffler, a snob, a coward - in a word, a man. And upon this rock He has built His Church, and the gates of Hell have not prevailed against it. All the empires and the kingdoms have failed, because of this inherent and continual weakness, that they were founded by strong men and upon strong men. But this one thing, the historic Christian Church, was founded on a weak man, and for that reason it is indestructible. For no chain is stronger than its weakest link."[63]

The most insidious threat to the ordinary man in our age, Chesterton believed, was from the philosophies of people like Bernard Shaw and H. G. Wells, who fiercely rejected their society for forcing men to live in squalid poverty, but who, in Chesterton's judgment, proposed measures which would abolish, not poverty, but man. Under socialism, as outlined by Shaw and Wells, every detail of human life would be closely regulated by the State; that is, by a massive bureaucracy. Chesterton gravely doubted whether this would ever satisfy the common man's fundamental needs - for instance, his need for freedom. "You have," he said, "left certain human needs out of your books; you may leave them out of your republic."[64]

Indeed, Chesterton considered that the growing tendency to see things in the mass, to cherish collectivist hopes, to think abstractly of "humanity" rather than of human beings, was doomed to destroy man in the end. He offered an appropriate reminder, that "because every man is a biped, fifty men are not a centipede."[65]

Combating a new slavery

The threat of slavery may not seem disturbingly serious in our time. It may be presumed that such a condition is only a feature of so-called under-developed nations or cultures. Yet to Chesterton and to his great friend, fellow Catholic and companion-in-arms, Hilaire Belloc, slavery was not only a permanent threat but one which is particularly formidable today, if perhaps more subtly so than in the past. In 1912, Belloc wrote **The Servile State**, a seminal work in which, as George Orwell, the author of *Animal Farm* and *1984*, acknowledged, he foretold "with remarkable insight the kind of things that have been happening from about 1930 onwards."[66]

The basic contention of this book, a magisterial interpretation of social history, is that modern economic systems, including the Welfare State, deprive the ordinary man both of the means of production and the fruits of production. The latter comprise not only wages but also property, since, in Pope Leo XIII's words, "when a man engages in remunerative labour, the impelling reason and motive of his work is to obtain property, and therefore to hold it as his very own".[67] Present-day systems destroy the ordinary person's economic freedom - and thereafter, by appallingly easy progression, his political freedom - by robbing him of the right to private ownership of property.

It is little, if any, compensation that individuals now enjoy an adequate standard of living. In the past, a society may well have been relatively comfortable; but it had still been enslaved. Were security and sufficiency to be preferred to freedom? Chesterton emphatically thought not, but he feared that the appetite for freedom, particularly in face of inconvenience, might be losing its appeal for modern people.

In a multitude of books, articles, lectures and debates, Chesterton unfolded his conception of an alternative society. The measures of social reform which he proposed were designed to restore dignity and freedom to the ordinary person. Unlike the socialists, Chesterton did not patronize the poor by advocating the distribution of money among them. He advocated the distribution of **power** - power in the form of property, as wide as possible a spread of property, with the laws designed to check any growth towards monopolization.

Chesterton's sociology was integrated with his theology; his beliefs about man flowed from his beliefs about God. In our time sociology has, in common with many disciplines, become largely secularized - divorced from theology and drained of its spiritual ramifications. In Chesterton there was no such rupture. He spoke as a citizen of the City of Man **and** of the City of God. His social philosophy was consistent with his religious outlook and mission, and formed, indeed, part of that outlook and mission. When he wrote to his mother to tell her of his conversion to Catholicism, he spoke of his conviction "that the fight for the family and the free citizen and everything decent must now be waged by [the] one fighting form of Christianity".[68] In his eyes the Church was not an ark of salvation in which the faithful might ride out the flood; it was rather a great dam by which they might combat the flood, and by restraining it, preserve the fertility of God's good earth.

Chesterton's Legacy

'The Everlasting Man'

The masterpiece of Chesterton's Catholic phase is **The Everlasting Man** (1925). When C. S. Lewis read it, he perceived for the first time the whole Christian outline of history, set out in an intelligible and convincing way.[69] In one sense **The Everlasting Man** is the fulfilment of **Orthodoxy**, for it extends and develops the thesis of that monumental work over the general field of human history.

The book is divided into two parts, "The Creature Called Man" and "The Man Called Christ". Its central contentions are brilliantly argued: first, that man, so far from being merely a particularly gifted kind of animal, is different in kind from the animal creation; second, that Jesus Christ, so far from being merely one of the great religious founders like Mohammed, is of a different order of being from other men; and third, that just as man is unique in the order of creation and Christ is unique in the human order, so the Catholic Church, which Christ founded, is unique among human institutions.

In a stimulating chapter called "The Five Deaths of the Faith", Chesterton insists that even the vicissitudes and apparent defeats which the Church has suffered in history confirm rather than contradict this general thesis. "Christianity," he declares, "has died many times and risen again; for it had a god who knew the way out of the grave."[70]

As the years lengthened, Chesterton's health began to weaken. More and more unmistakably did he show signs of mounting strain and fatigue.

Only three years before his death, he produced a biography of **St Thomas Aquinas** (1933). The distinguished philosopher, Etienne Gilson, acclaimed it "as being without possible comparison the best book ever written on St. Thomas".[71] Its basic premise is that St. Thomas is, pre-eminently, the philosopher of common sense - in a world, as Chesterton asserted elsewhere, where sense is no longer common.[72] The principles of Thomistic philosophy, argued Chesterton, rest upon, and also reinforce, the axioms and intuitions which ordinary people accept; they begin with facts of everyday experience, like the existence of motion, and not with highly debatable assumptions or "funny internal feelings" which cannot be shared.

Childlikeness

Thus, in the twilight of his life, Chesterton came again to emphasize the importance and enchantment of the ordinary life - the life of order and normality. He understood this life because he had lived it himself. His greatness as a writer was matched by his greatness as a man. Goodness and wisdom were combined in him to a remarkable degree. With great dedication did he practise the Augustinian precept to destroy errors but love men. Few individuals more naturally distinguished between a man and his views, or found easier the theological injunction to hate the sin but love the sinner.

His contemporaries found in him a living example of charity and humility and childlike innocence. What has often been misconstrued as childishness was, in fact, *childlikeness* - reflecting a basic humility of nature and a simplicity and clarity of mind. Chesterton was the living exemplar of Christ's injunction that "unless you be converted and become as little children, you shall not enter into the Kingdom of Heaven".[73]

The humorous side of this attribute was expressed, firstly, in his sharp wit. When one interviewer asked him what single book he would choose if cast on a desert island, he replied Thomas's **Guide to Practical Shipbuilding**. Secondly, it was conveyed in his sublime absentmindedness. There is the now legendary telegram which he sent his wife on one occasion when he had gone to fulfil a lecturing engagement: "Am in Market Harborough. Where ought I to be?" Of course, "absence of mind", as Chesterton himself saw it, really means presence of mind on something else; and it is clear that no person engaged in creative work can be constantly aware of the round of daily life, least of all a person as continuously and prodigiously creative as Chesterton was.

The serious influence of his childlikeness was manifest in his remarkable power of prophecy. He was a man of exceptional vision, who read the signs of our times with penetrating clarity - the clarity of a child seeing something for the first time. He saw things in the light of eternity rather than of time, and was able to gauge the future importance of evils which were, at the time, barely discernible.

Chesterton the prophet

One of the passionate concerns of his life was the assaults which modern culture had mounted upon human dignity and nature. Believing that man bears the imprint of his Creator, a source which gives him a sacred and inviolable nature, Chesterton resisted mightily the modern tendency to alter human nature to fit conditions, instead of altering conditions to fit human nature. Long before the advances in genetic engineering which have taken place in our time, Chesterton realised that, when once man began to be viewed as a shifting and provisional and alterable thing, it would always be easy for the strong and the clever to twist him into new shapes for all kinds of unnatural purposes. If man's nature is not fixed and elevated by God beyond human interference, then there is nothing to prevent the powerful from adapting it, fundamentally and endlessly.

What is to prevent, Chesterton asked, the new marvels turning into the old abuses - the old abuses of debasement and slavery? "That is the nightmare with which the mere notion of adaptation threatens us," he wrote in 1910, in his major work of Christian sociology, **What's Wrong with the World**. "That is the nightmare that is not so very far from the reality."[74] A century later, it is clear how alarmingly close to reality that nightmare is.

Another remarkable instance of Chesterton's insight was his prophecy of Liberalism, which he saw was tending towards something very different from what it envisaged. "The earnest Freethinkers," predicted Chesterton in 1905, "need not worry themselves so much about the persecutions of the past. Before the Liberal idea is dead or triumphant, we shall see wars and persecutions the like of which the world has never seen."[75] Citing these words more than half a century later, Malcolm Muggeridge noted that, in 1905, Stalin was but a young man of twenty-six, and Hitler ten years younger, and they were, along with others, to fulfil Chesterton's prophecy to a terrifying degree.[76] At the outbreak of World War II, T. S. Eliot reflected Chesterton's prophecy in his conclusion that Liberalism is preparing "the way for that which is its own negation: the artificial, mechanised or brutalised control which is a desperate remedy for its chaos".[77]

Chesterton died on 14th June, 1936, barely a month after his sixty-second birthday. At his funeral his faithful ally, Hilaire Belloc, was heard muttering distractedly: "Chesterton will never occur again."[78]

Yet his thought - and the example of his life - remains an imperishable legacy. Chesterton perceived that we were entering a period in human history when Western people would reject not only God, but man; not only the supernatural, but the natural. "And those of us," he wrote in defence of marriage in 1920,

> "who have seen all the normal rules and relations of humanity uprooted by random speculators, as if they were abnormal abuses and almost accidents, will understand why men have sought for something divine if they wished to preserve anything human. They will know why common sense, cast out from some academy of fads and fashions conducted on the lines of a luxurious madhouse, has age after age sought refuge in the high sanity of a sacrament."[79]

Yet the march of spiritual and intellectual destruction, predicted Chesterton, would continue space.

> "Everything will be denied. Everything will become a creed . . . Fires will be kindled to testify that two and two make four. Swords will be drawn to prove

that leaves are green in summer. We shall be left defending, not only the incredible virtues and sanities of human life, but something more incredible still, this huge impossible universe which stares us in the face. We shall fight for visible prodigies as if they were invisible. We shall look on the impossible grass and the skies with a strange courage. We shall be of those who have seen and yet have believed."[80]

Further reading

A major resurgence of interest in G.K. Chesterton has taken place in recent decades. There has been a continuing flow of biographical studies, including Joseph Pearce's *Wisdom and Innocence: A Life of G.K. Chesterton* (1996), Dale Ahlquist's *G.K. Chesterton: the Apostle of Common Sense* (2003), and Aidan Mackey's *G.K. Chesterton: A Prophet for the 21st Century* (2007), as well as a reprint of the classic work, Maisie Ward's *Gilbert Keith Chesterton*.

The bulk of Chesterton's most popular books have been reprinted, either as single titles or as part of a *Collected Works of G.K. Chesterton* project undertaken by the American publisher, Ignatius Press. Anthologies have also appeared, such as *The Bodley Head G.K. Chesterton* (1985).

The G.K. Chesterton Institute for Faith & Culture at Seton Hall University (New Jersey, USA) has established an international presence, organising conferences in countries as diverse as England, Croatia and Argentina, and publishing a substantial quarterly journal, *The Chesterton Review*, edited by Fr Ian Boyd CSB. Both the Review and the *Collected Works* have brought to light many unconsolidated or elusive pieces of Chesterton's writings, providing fresh evidence of his vast and extravagant talent.

Societies have also been formed in various countries, particularly the United States as well as England, Latin America and Australia. The American Chesterton Society has been the most adventurously active, publishing a regular journal, *Gilbert Magazine*, presenting a regular television series on EWTN, and conducting an annual conference in St Paul, Minnesota.

Endnotes

[1] Introduction to G. K. Chesterton, *Autobiography*, new ed., 1969, p. 7.

[2] *The Georgian Literary Scene*, revised ed., 1969, p. 82.

[3] "Fairy Tales," in *All Things Considered*, 3rd ed., 1908, p. 256.

[4] *ibid.*, p. 257.

[5] "Behind the Toby Jug," *Observer* (London), 13th April, 1969, p. 28.

[6] Quoted in Maisie Ward, Gilbert Keith Chesterton, 1944, p. 42.

[7] *ibid.*, p. 26.

[8] Quoted in A. L. Maycock (ed.), *The Man Who Was Orthodox*, 1963, p. 15.

[9] *The Defendant*, 1901, p. 16.

[10] "G. K. Chesterton," in P. Caraman (ed.), *Occasional Sermons of Ronald A. Knox*, 1960, p. 404.

[11] "The Shop of Ghosts: A Good Dream," in *Tremendous Trifles*, 1909, p. 249.

[12] "Literary London," in *G. K. C. as M. C.*, 1929, p. 33.

[13] *Father Malachy's Miracle*, new ed., 1947, p.6.

[14] Maycock, *op. cit.*, p. 170.

[15] Maycock, *op. cit.*, p. 160.

[16] *What I Saw in America*, 1922, p. 33.

[17] *Tremendous Trifles*, 1909, p. 68.

[18] "Cecil Chesterton," in *G. K. C. as M. C.*, 1929, p. 117.

[19] In 1944 Miss Ward produced an authoritative biography of Chesterton, *Gilbert Keith Chesterton*. So enormous was the response to it that, in 1952, she composed a sequel, *Return to Chesterton*.

[20] "The Three Kinds of Men," in *Alarms and Discursions*, 5th ed., 1927, p. 149.

[21] In the 1960s, disquiet about population growth led to proposals for draconian measures, sponsored by scientists like Paul Ehrlich, author of *The Population Bomb* (1968). More recently, the concerns about climate change have given new stimulus to anti-human ideologies. As reported by the London *Catholic Herald* (February 1, 2008), an Australian medical academic has advocated a carbon tax on children for the

damage they inflict on the environment, replacing the baby bonus currently provided. Cardinal George Pell of Sydney criticised the proposal as 'a striking illustration of where a minority, neo-pagan, anti-human mentality wants to take us."

[22] Quoted in M. Ward, *Gilbert Keith Chesterton*, 1944, p. 538.
[23] *Orthodoxy*, 1908, p. 96.
[24] *ibid*, p. 151.
[25] Quoted in M. Ward, *Gilbert Keith Chesterton*, 1944, p. 140.
[26] *Mere Christianity*, 1952, p. 118.
[27] "How It All Began," *Tablet* (London), 8th February, 1969, p. 132.
[28] Dawn Eden, *The Thrill of the Chaste: Finding Fulfilment While Keeping Your Clothes on* (2006), and "Casual sex is a con: women just aren't like men," *Sunday Times* (London), 14 January 2007.
[29] *Orthodoxy*, 1908, p. 184-5.
[30] *Orthodoxy*, 1908, p. 17.
[31] *A Short History of England*, new ed., 1929, p. viii.
[32] *The Common Man*, 1950, p. 22.
[33] J. H. Newman, *Apologia Pro Vita Sua*, 1864, p. 242.
[34] *The Thing*, 1929, p. 227.
[35] Quoted in M. Ward, *Gilbert Keith Chesterton*, 1944, p. 176.
[36] *Orthodoxy*, 1908, p. 141.
[37] *The Surprise*, 1952, p. 63.
[38] *Illustrated London News*, 6th July, 1935, p. 6.
[39] *ibid*.
[40] *Now I See*, 1933, p. 76.
[41] *Orthodoxy*, 1908, p. 12.
[42] Quoted in M. Ward, *Gilbert Keith Chesterton*, 1944, p. 177.
[43] *G. K. C. as M. C.*, 1929, p. 42.
[44] *Autobiography*, 1936, p. 158.
[45] *Collected Poems*, 1933, p. 387.
[46] *The Thing*, 1929, p. 20.
[47] *Blackfriars*, March 1923. Quoted in A. L. Maycock (ed.), op. cit., p. 183.
[48] W. H. Auden (ed.), *G. K. Chesterton; a selection from his non-fictional prose*, 1970, p. 13.

50

[49] Quoted in R. Kojecky, *T. S. Eliot's Social Criticism*, 1972, p. 87.

[50] *G. K. C. as M. C.*, 1929, p. xiv.

[51] Kingsley Amis (ed.), *G. K. Chesterton; selected stories*, 1972, p. 18. It is a curious fact that, as Catholics neglected Chesterton in the period following the 1960s, either out of embarrassment at his pre-Vatican II Catholicism or for other reasons, non-Catholics began to resurrect him – W. H. Auden, an Anglo-Catholic, for example, and Kingsley Amis, an agnostic. More recently, converts to Catholicism have been among his most prominent advocates – such as Dale Ahlquist, President of the American Chesterton Society, who came from an Evangelical Protestant background, and Joseph Pearce, the author of many biographies, including *Wisdom and Innocence: A Life of G.K. Chesterton* (1996), who attributes to Chesterton his conversion from agnosticism to Catholicism.

[52] He also produced a portrait of his friend, *Father Brown on Chesterton*, 1937.

[53] W. W. Robson, "G. K. Chesterton's '*Father Brown*' Stories," *Southern Review* (U.S.A.), Summer 1969, p. 618.

[54] *The Innocence of Father Brown*, 1911, p. 234.

[55] *The Innocence of Father Brown*, 1911, p. 186.

[56] Dorothy Collins (ed.), *Chesterton on Shakespeare*, 1971, p. 159.

[57] *The Everlasting Man*, 1925, p. 9.

[58] *Victorian Age in Literature*, 1912, pp. 39-40.

[59] *G. K. C. as M. C.*, 1929, p. 114.

[60] *G. K.'s; a miscellany of the first 500 issues of 'G. K.'s Weekly'*, 1934, p. 50.

[61] Quoted in M. Ward, *Gilbert Keith Chesterton*, 1944, p. 358.

[62] Quoted in A. L. Maycock (ed.), op. cit., p. 30.

[63] *Heretics*, 1905, pp. 60-1.

[64] Quoted in M. Ward, *Return to Chesterton*, 1952, p. 58.

[65] *What's Wrong with the World*, 1910, p. 4.

[66] George Orwell, *Collected Essays*, 1961, p.371.

[67] *Rerum Novarum*, art. 5.

[68] Quoted in M. Ward, *Gilbert Keith Chesterton*, 1944, p. 397

[69] *Surprised by Joy*, new ed., 1959, p. 178.

[70] *The Everlasting Man*, 1925, p. 288.

[71] Quoted in C. Clemens, *G. K. Chesterton*, 1939, pp. 150-1.

[72] *G. K. C. as M. C.*, 1929, p. 266.

[73] Matthew, XVIII, 3.

[74] *What's Wrong with the World*, 1910, p. 260.

[75] *Daily News*, 18th February, 1905; reprinted in A. L. Maycock (ed.), op. cit., p. 123.

[76] "G.K.C.," *New Statesman*, 23 August 1963, p.226. Repr. In Malcolm Muggeridge, *Things Past*, ed. Ian Hunter, 1978, p.148. Muggeridge also commented that, while Chesterton has so often been proved right in his judgments, it is surprising that he should still be less seriously regarded than 'prophets' at the time like H.G. Wells, who were almost invariably wrong.

[77] *Idea of a Christian Society*, 1939, p. 12.

[78] Robert Speaight, *Life of Hilaire Belloc*, 1957, p. 481.

[79] *The Superstition of Divorce*, 1920, p. 146.

[80] *Heretics*, 1905, pp. 307-8.

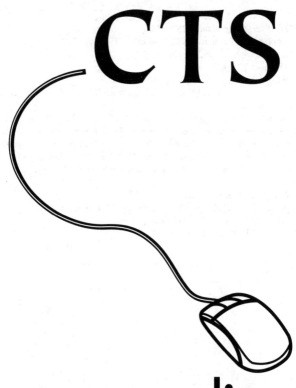

CTS

... now online
www.cts-online.org.uk